ANDREA CAPPELLARI

FIRST BOOK
OF CLASSICAL VIOLIN

T0087140

VIOLIN

To access companion recorded accompaniments
online, visit:
www.halleonard.com/mylibrary

Enter Code
4557-2257-0892-6244

ISBN 978-1-5400-5460-9

RICORDI

EXCLUSIVELY DISTRIBUTED BY

Visit Hal Leonard Online at
www.halleonard.com

Contact us:
Hal Leonard
7777 West Bluemound Road
Milwaukee, WI 53213
Email: info@halleonard.com

In Europe, contact:
Hal Leonard Europe Limited
42 Wigmore Street
Marylebone, London, W1U 2RN
Email: info@halleonardeurope.com

In Australia, contact:
Hal Leonard Australia Pty. Ltd.
4 Lentara Court
Cheltenham, Victoria, 3192 Australia
Email: info@halleonard.com.au

Andrea Cappellari holds degrees in choral music and choral conducting, music education, and percussion instruments from the Giuseppe Verdi Conservatory in Milan. He is a lecturer at the Giacomo Puccini Higher Institute of Music Studies in Gallarate, Varese, Italy, and at the Candiani-Bausch High School of the Arts in Busto Arsizio, Varese, Italy. He teaches training and continuing education courses for teachers and courses in rhythm and ensemble music in French-speaking Switzerland. He is a director of choral and instrumental ensembles, and author of numerous educational publications and collections of children's songs.

In memory of my beloved mother Wanda.

Thanks to Giusy Tunici, Federico Curioni

Cover Art by Giuseppe Spada

CONTENTS

MELODIES INDEXED BY COMPOSER

1 **Melodies of 3 Notes/Rhythmic Values:** 𝅝 𝅗𝅥. 𝅗𝅥 𝅘𝅥

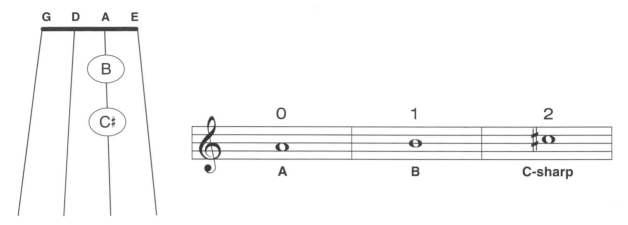

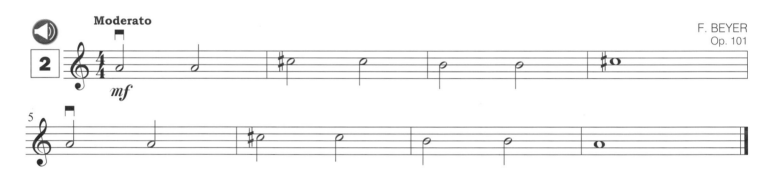

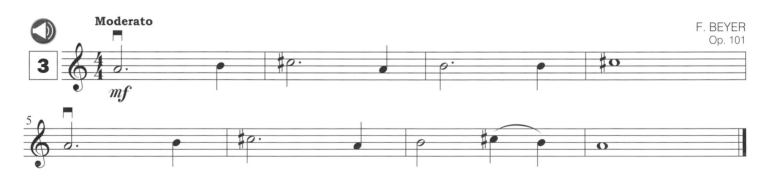

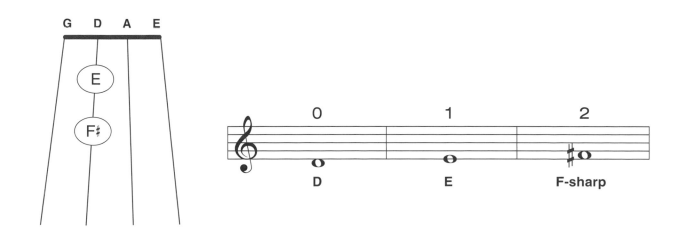

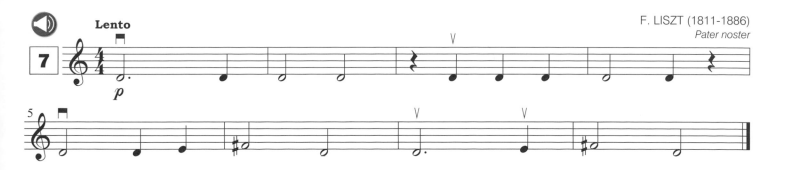

2 Melodies of 4 Notes/Rhythmic Values: o o. o o

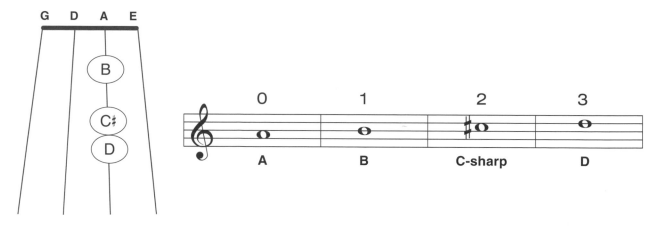

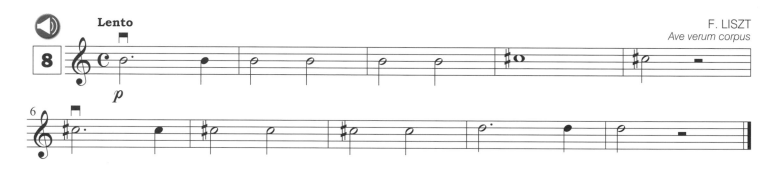

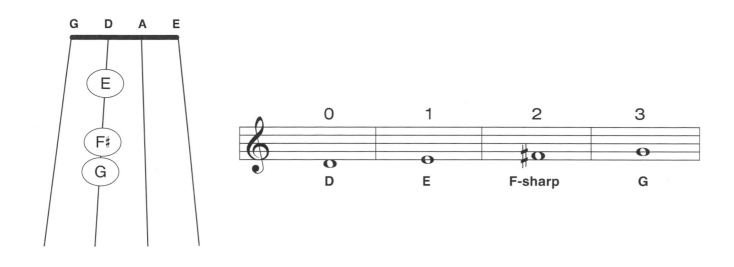

Melodies of 5 Notes/Rhythmic Values: from 𝅝 to ♪

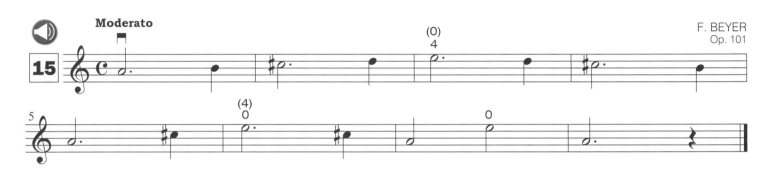

F. BEYER
Op. 101

N. HERMAN (1500 -1560)
Aus meines Herzens Grunde

G.F. HANDEL (1685 -1759)
Sing ye to the Lord (Israel in Aegypt)

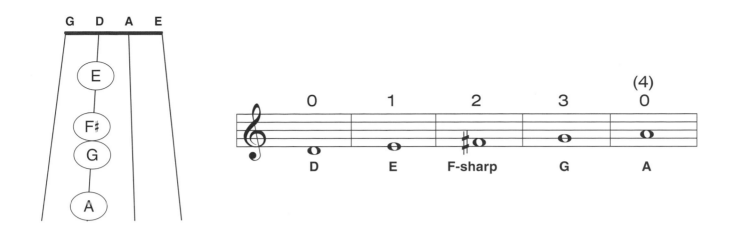

Andante con moto   (4)   A. FOOTE (1853 -1937)
Quite contented

18

Andantino   A. FOOTE
Waltz

19

Animato   A. SCHMOLL
Petit Étude

20

4 Melodies of 6 Notes/Rhythmic Values: from o to ♪

5 Melodies of 6 Notes/Rhythmic Values: from 𝅝 to ♪

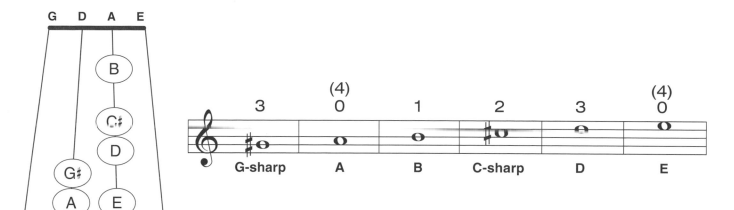

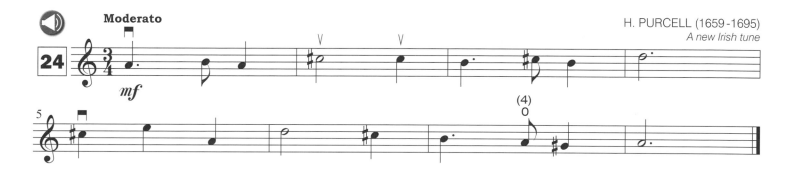

Moderato

H. PURCELL (1659-1695)
A new Irish tune

24

Menuetto grazioso

I. PLEYEL (1757-1831)
Sonatina n. 6

25

Andante

A. FOOTE
Reverie

26

6 A-Major Scale

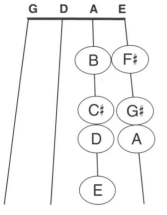

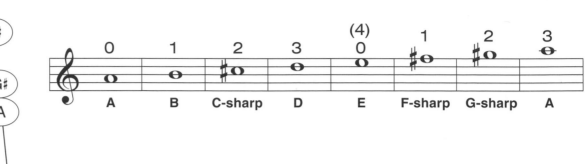

A   B   C-sharp   D   E   F-sharp   G-sharp   A

I. PLEYEL
Rondò - Sonatina n. 1

C. FRANCK
Domine non secundum

G. LANGE (1830 - 1889)
Arietta - Sonatina Op. 114 n. 4

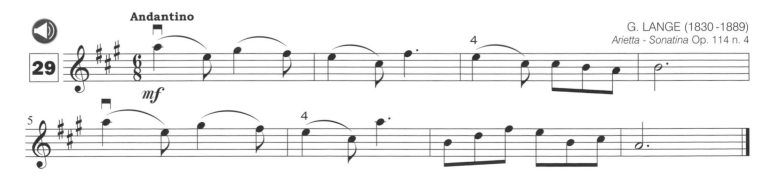

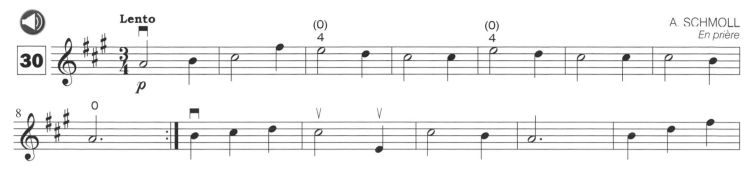

A. SCHMOLL
En prière

Lento

30

F. BURGMÜLLER (1806-1874)
Ave Maria

Andantino

31

W.L. HAYDEN
Rondò

Andante

32

7 D-Major Scale

N. PORPORA (1686-1768)
Concerto IV

Allegro

33

mf

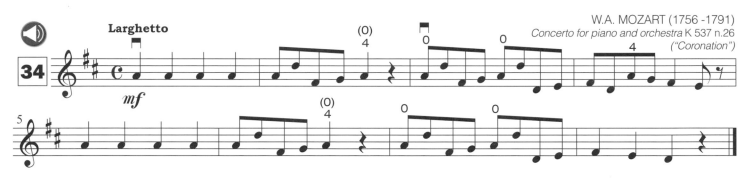

W.A. MOZART (1756-1791)
Concerto for piano and orchestra K 537 n.26
("Coronation")

Larghetto

34

mf

L.E. GEBHARDI (1787-1862)
Der Sommerabend

Lento

35

mf

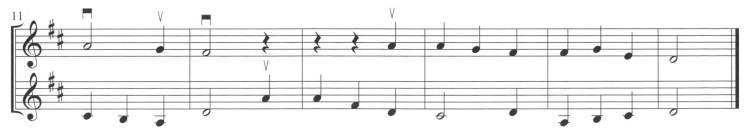

Anonymous (18th Century)
Magnificat

36

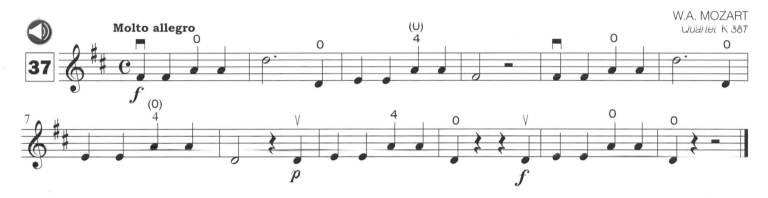

W.A. MOZART
Quartet K.387

37

N. PORPORA
Concerto IV

38

L.E. GEBHARDI
Wasserlied

39

* Optional: C♮

Melodies of 3 Notes/Rhythmic Values:

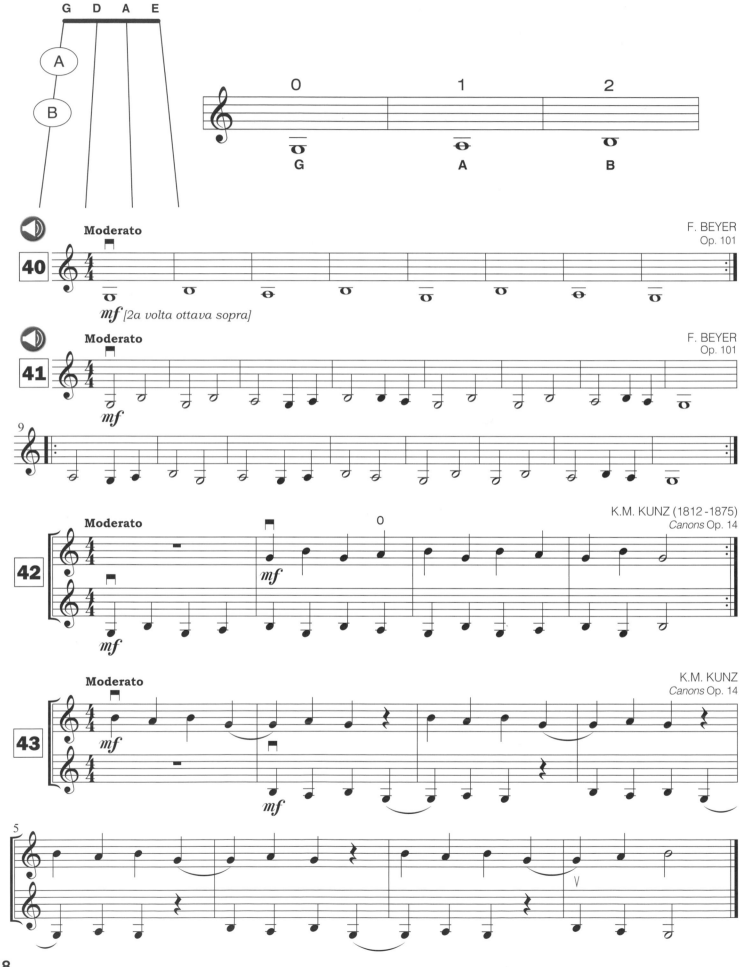

F. BEYER
Op. 101

mf [2a volta ottava sopra]

F. BEYER
Op. 101

K.M. KUNZ (1812-1875)
Canons Op. 14

K.M. KUNZ
Canons Op. 14

FIRST BOOK OF CLASSICAL VIOLIN

F. BEYER (1803-1863) Op. 101

F. BEYER Op. 101

F. BEYER Op. 101

F. BEYER Op. 101

F. BEYER Op. 101

F. BEYER Op. 101

6 Moderato

7 Lento

F. LISZT (1811-1886) *Pater noster*

8 Lento

F. LISZT *Ave verum corpus*

9 Moderato

F. BEYER Op. 101

10 Moderato

F. BEYER Op. 101

F. BEYER Op. 101

Moderato

F. BEYER Op. 101

Moderato

A. SCHMOLL (1841-1931) *Petit Étude*

Andantino

M. HAYDN (1737-1806) *In dir ruht, Herr*

Moderato

F. BEYER Op. 101

15 Moderato

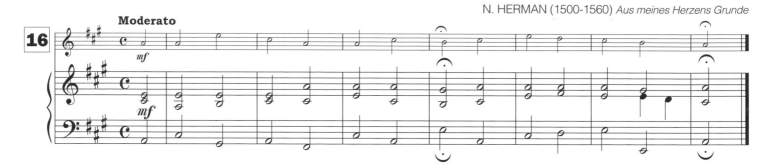

N. HERMAN (1500-1560) *Aus meines Herzens Grunde*

16 Moderato

G.F. HANDEL (1685-1759) *Sing ye to the Lord (Isreal in Aegypt)*

17 A tempo giusto

12

A. FOOTE (1853-1937) *Quite contented*

18 Andante con moto

7

A. FOOTE *Waltz*

A. SCHMOLL *Petit Étude*

F. MENDELSSOHN (1809-1847) *Laudate pueri*

22 Maestoso ma non lento

C. FRANCK (1822-1890) *Dextera Domini*

23 Moderato

W.L. HAYDEN (1839-1886) *Waltz*

24 Moderato

H. PURCELL (1659-1695) *A new Irish tune*

25 Menuetto grazioso

I. PLEYEL (1757-1831) *Sonatina* n. 6

26 **Andante**

A. FOOTE *Reverie*

27 **Moderato**

I. PLEYEL *Sonatina n. 1*

28 **Andante non troppo**

C. FRANCK *Domine non secundum*

G. LANGE (1830-1889) *Arietta - Sonatina* Op. 114 n. 4

29 Andantino

A. SCHMOLL (1841-1931)
En prière

30 Lento

F. BURGMÜLLER (1806-1874) *Ave Maria*

31 Andantino

W.L. HAYDEN *Rondò*

32 Andante

N. PORPORA (1686 - 1768) *Concerto IV*

33 Allegro

34 Larghetto   W.A. MOZART (1756-1791) *Concerto for piano and orchestra* K 537 n. 26 *("Coronation")*

36 [Andante]   Anonymous (18th century) *Magnificat*

37 Molto allegro   W.A. MOZART *Quartet* K 387

40 Moderato   F. BEYER Op. 101

Moderato

49   B. SMETANA (1824-1884)

Moderato

51   F. SCHUBERT (1797-1886) *Tänze Serie 12 n. 1*

Allegretto   *Fine*   F. BEYER Op. 101

53

D.C. al Fine

Andante   F. BEYER Op. 101

54

[Andante moderato]   G. GASTOLDI (1555-1622) *La Cortigiana*

55

[Moderato]   D. MANZOLO (17th century)

56

12

A. DIABELLI (1781-1858) *Alla turca*

A. FOOTE *A little Waltz*

66 Lento   M.A. CHARPENTIER (1634-1704) *Domine Deus (Messe de minuit)*

67 Moderato   J. PACHELBEL (1653-1706) *Gott ist unser Zuversicht*

68 Adagio religioso   J. BERANEK (1813-1875) *Pater noster*

69 Allegro   W.A. MOZART *Deutsche Tänze - Serie 11 n. 13*

70 Presto   A. DVOŘÁK (1841-1904) *Slavanic Dance* Op. 46 n. 1

Allegro moderato

77

Comodo

78

Comodo

79

Moderato

80

81 F. BEYER Op. 101

82 F. BEYER Op. 101

83 M. LUTHER (1483-1546) *Nun freut euch*

84 W.A. MOZART *Menuetto* (Serie 24 n. 58)

85 M. HAYDN *Kommt, ihr Christen*

86 Vivace

87 Moderato

88 Allegretto

89 Andante

90 Andante

94

Brillante e vivace

95

Melodioso

96

Assai vivo

100

Non troppo veloce

9 Melodies of 5 Notes/Rhythmic Values: from 𝅗𝅥. to ♪

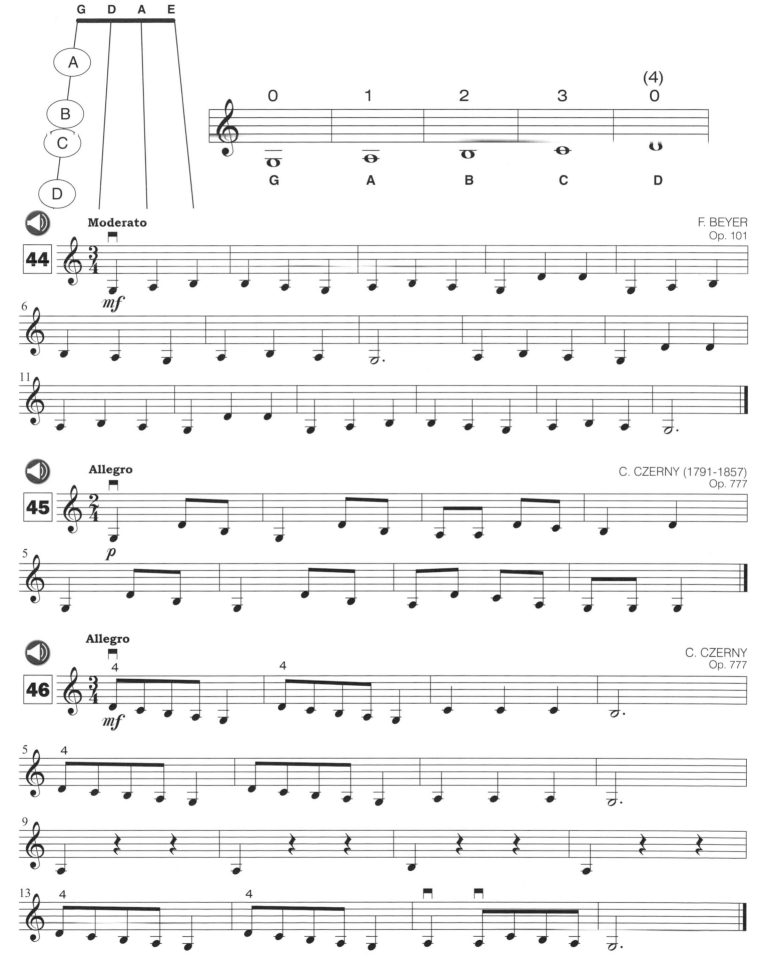

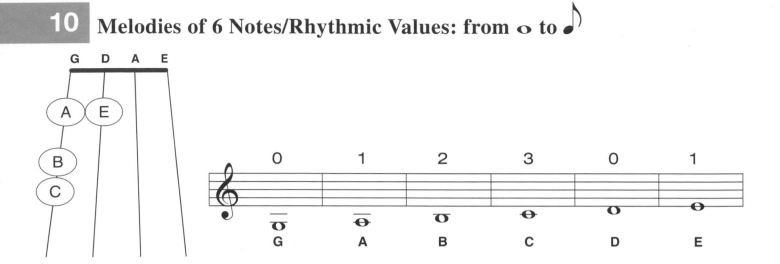

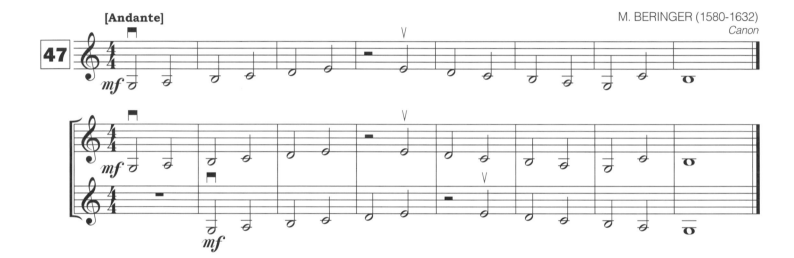

[Andante]

M. BERINGER (1580-1632)
Canon

47

[Andante moderato]

M. BERINGER
Canon

48

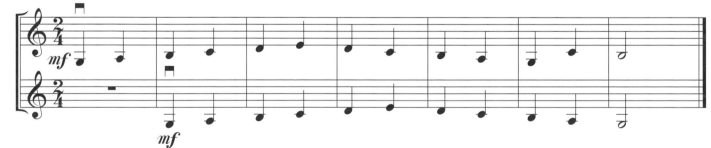

Moderato

B. SMETANA (1824-1884)

49

11 G-Major Scale

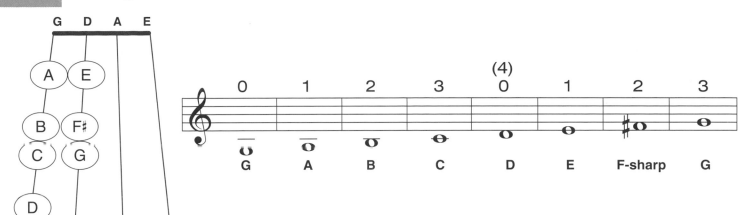

L.E. GEBHARDI
2-Part Canon

F. SCHUBERT (1797-1828)
Tänze Serie 12 n. 1

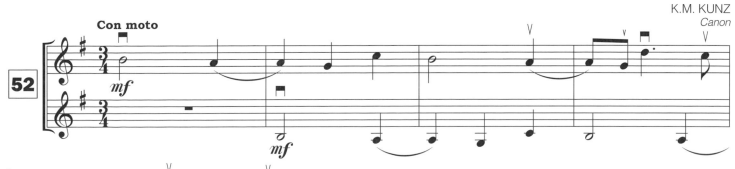

K.M. KUNZ
Canon

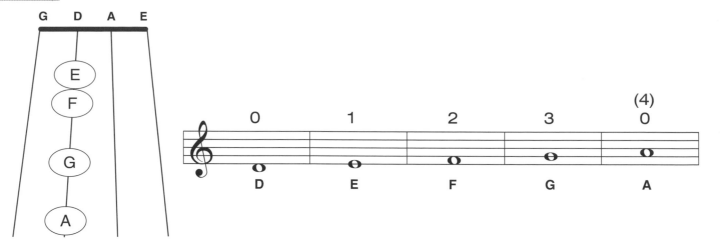

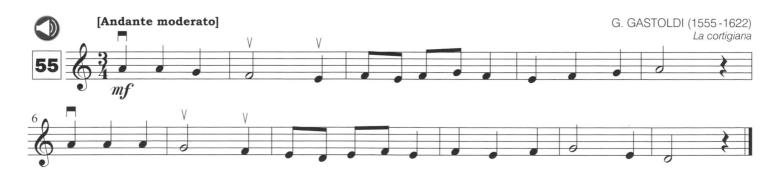

56 [Moderato] D. MANZOLO (17th Century)

57 Allegro A. DIABELLI (1781-1858)
Alla turca

58 Allegro A. FOOTE
A little Waltz

13 Melodies of 5 Notes/Rhythmic Values: from 𝅗𝅥. to ♪

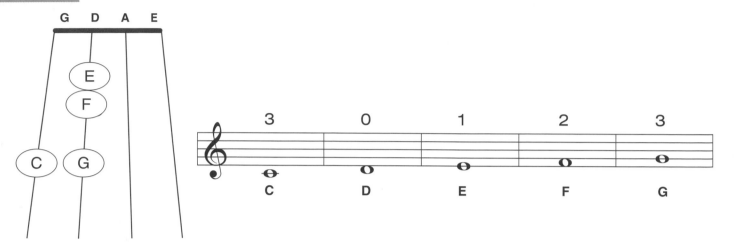

A. SCHMOLL
Petit Étude

Un poco animato

59

p

A. CORELLI (1653-1713)
Concerto grosso n. 1

Largo

60

mf

M. CORRETTE (1707-1795)
Menuet allemand

[Allegretto]

61

mf

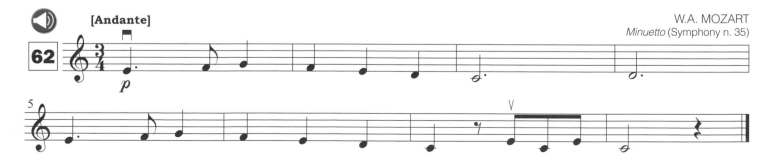

W.A. MOZART
Minuetto (Symphony n. 35)

[Andante]

62

p

24

14 Melodies of 5 Notes/Rhythmic Values: from 𝅝 to ♪

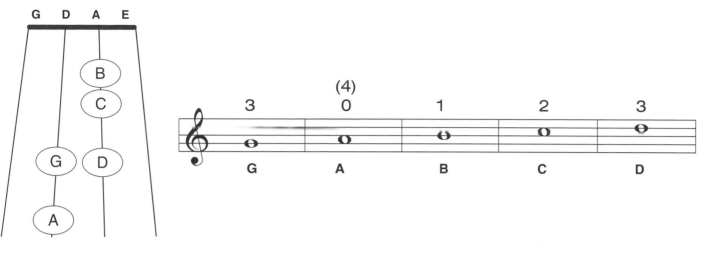

F. BEYER
Op. 101

G.F. HANDEL
Concerto grosso Op. 6 n. 11

J. ROSENMÜLLER (1619-1684)
Meine Seele harret auf Gott

M.A. CHARPENTIER (1634-1704)
Domine Deus (Messe de minuit)

15 C-Major Scale

71
A. CALDARA (1670-1736)
Penso e ripenso

72
M. HAYDN
Wie trostreich

73
L.E. GEBHARDI
Morgengesang

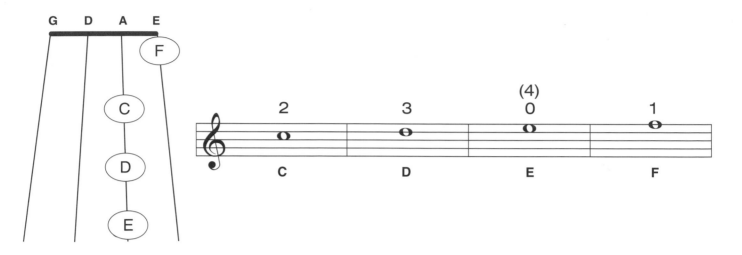

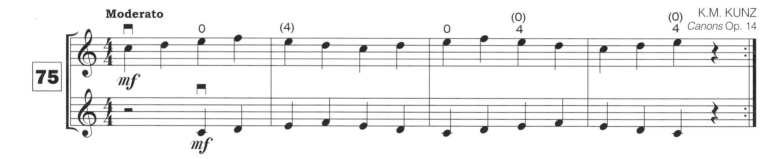

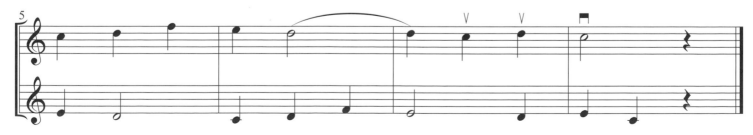

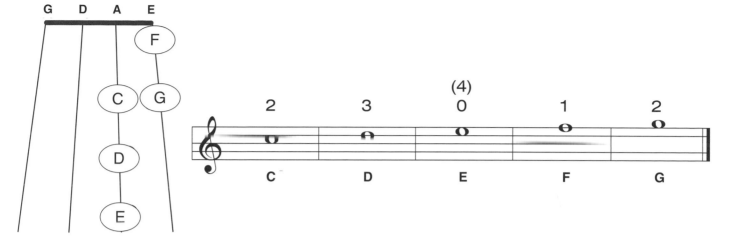

18 Melodies of 5 Notes/Rhythmic Values: from 𝅝 to ♪

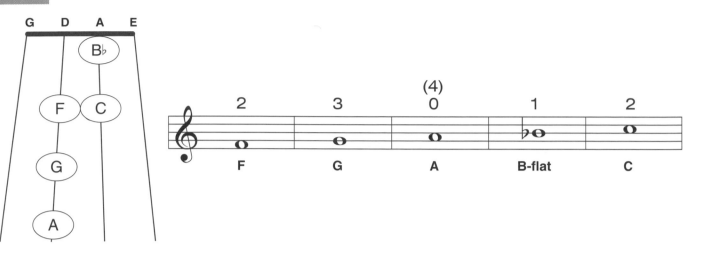

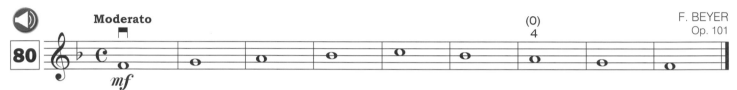

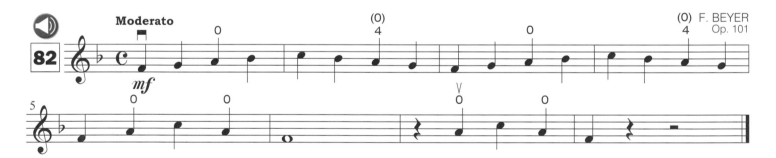

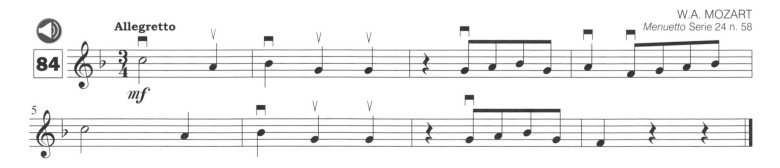

85 Moderato

M. HAYDN
Kommt, ihr Christen

86 Vivace

A. CAMPRA (1660-1744)
Jubilate Deo

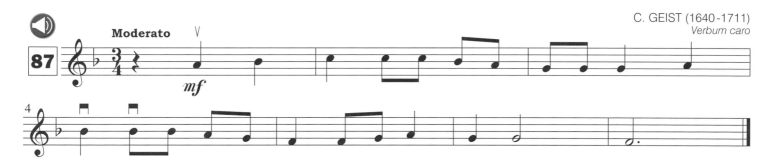

87 Moderato

C. GEIST (1640-1711)
Verbum caro

88 Allegretto

C. CZERNY
Op. 777

19 Melodies of 6 Notes/Rhythmic Values: from 𝅝 to 𝅘𝅥𝅮

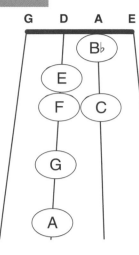

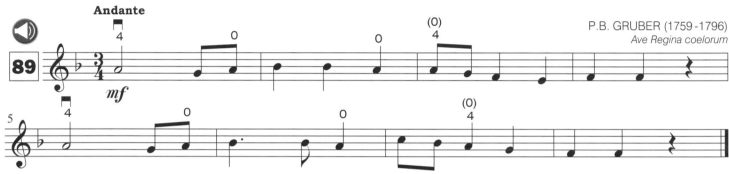

1	2	3	(4)\n0	1	2
E	F	G	A	B-flat	C

P.B. GRUBER (1759 -1796)
Ave Regina coelorum

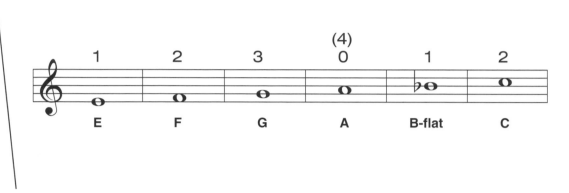

89

M.A. CHARPENTIER
Klein Te Deum

90

W.A. MOZART
Deutsche Tänze - Serie 11 n. 13

91

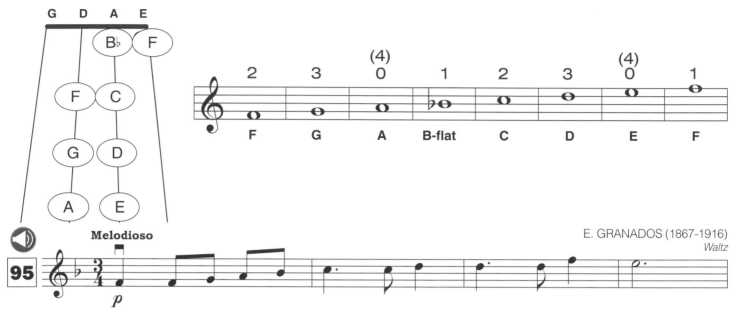

F G A B-flat C D E F

Melodioso

E. GRANADOS (1867-1916)
Waltz

95

Assai vivo

A. SCHMOLL
Petit Étude

96

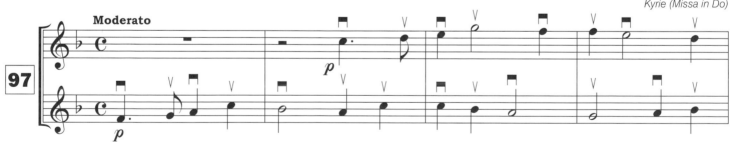

B. GALUPPI (1706-1785)
Kyrie (Missa in Do)

Moderato

97

B. GALUPPI
Sanctus (Missa in Do)

98

L.E. GEBHARDI
Vaterlandsliebe

99

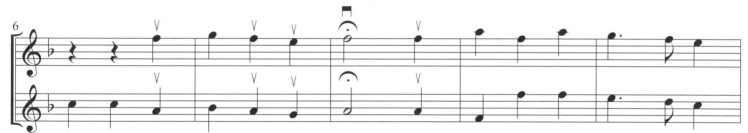

M.A. CHARPENTIER
Vous qui désirez sans fin

100

GLOSSARY

A tempo giusto	*In strict tempo*
Adagio religioso	*Slow, devotional*
Allegretto	*Fairly quick*
Allegro	*Fast*
Allegro moderato	*Moderately fast*
Andante	*Walking tempo*
Andante con moto	*Walking tempo with motion*
Andante moderato	*Moderate walking tempo*
Andante non troppo	*Walking tempo not too much*
Andantino	*Close to walking tempo*
Animato	*Animatedly*
Assai vivo	*Very lively*
Brillante e vivace	*Brilliant and lively*
Comodo	*Comfortably*
Con moto	*With motion*
Larghetto	*A little broad*
Largo	*Broad*
Lento	*Slow*
Maestoso ma non lento	*Majestic but not slow*
Melodioso	*Singing*
Menuetto grazioso	*Graceful minuet*
Moderato	*Moderately*
Molto allegro	Very quick
Non troppo veloce	*Not too rapidly*
Presto	*Very fast*
Un poco animato	*A little animated*
Vivace	*Lively*